DEDICATED

With the greatest respect
and appreciation to my
family, who gave me so
much reinforcement, the
Deadwood rain that kept
me inside to write recipes
and cook, and mostly to my
son Joey, who ate the soups
with me.

CHRISTINA ANN WILBUR

CHRISTINA ANN WILBUR

# Deadwood Soups

## by Christina Ann Wilbur

## 25 Great Soups

*plus*

Seasonings • Stock • Thickenings

Garnishes • Croutons • Dumplings • Noodles

### IN MEMORY
#### Christina Ann Wilbur
#### January 4, 1950 — May 15, 2008

### PUBLISHER'S NOTE
We scanned the original pages of Chrissy's 1977 cookbook,
which she typeset, illustrated, and duplicated herself,
and added some favorite photos.

❦

Enjoy these recipes and the loving spirit of Chris Wilbur
who filled our lives with loud laughter, bawdy
surprises, companionship, and great soup.

## Deadwood Soups by Christina Ann Wilbur

### SECOND EDITION
ISBN: 978-0-9673025-4-6

First Edition was self-published by Chris Wilbur
in November 1977.

Second Edition re-released in May 2008 by Wyatt and
MacKenzie, to honor their Grandma Chris.

### Wyatt-MacKenzie Publishing, Inc.
#### DEADWOOD, OREGON

www.wymacpublishing.com

## INTRODUCTION

This book is about soups.  About soups, my family, and Deadwood.  Many years ago my ancestors came to Deadwood and homesteaded this land.  What they found here was timber, beautiful land, and of course, rain.  They cut the timber for their home, cleared and plowed the land for gardens orchards and pastures.  Life in those days were hard working, big eating, and very rewarding.  Families were close.  Usually they worked together and ate together.  This would mean a very big hot soup to warm them up after a day in the rain.  I remember large family gatherings and large tureens of soup.

In this book I've tried to put together some of the recipes that my great-grandmother, grandmother, and mother made.  I still like to fix a hot bowl of soup at the end of a cold winter day.

Oh, by the way, the reason I don't have that many cold soup recipes is because we don't have all that many hot days in Deadwood.

Good luck, and I hope you enjoy your book as much as I've enjoyed putting it together for you.

Chris Wilbur

C H R I S T I N A   A N N   W I L B U R

## TABLE OF CONTENTS

CHRISTINA ANN WILBUR

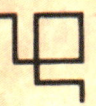

## SEASONINGS

To many soups, it's the stock that
makes or breaks it.  I always keep a
brown stock in the frig. for instant
use.  You know what they say, "Always
be prepared". The addition of wine also
enhances the flavor, but be careful
not to oversalt. Don't use more than 1/4
cup of wine to 1 quart soup.Also, don't
boil after adding the wine. When using
herbs and spices, don't be timid.Be
outrageous! (Heavy on the spices) Sour
cream, wine, butter, salt and pepper
and garlic are all necessities. Never
run out of any of these in your kitchen.

C H R I S T I N A   A N N   W I L B U R

## THICKENINGS

### RAW CEREALS

Rice, Oatmeal, Wheat Germ, Quick cooking tapioca. Stir in these in the last hour of cooking. You can also use flour, soya flour, wheat flour, or peanut flour.

### EGG YOLKS

This is the richest, but you must be careful that the soup is not too hot. (Way below the boiling point)The reason being is that it will curdle. I always use about 2 egg yolks per 1 1/2 cups soup stock. Serve immediately.

### GRATED RAW POTATOES

Add to stews, or potato  soups.

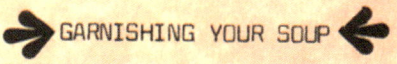 GARNISHING YOUR SOUP

<u>Always garnish</u>! You know how nice
it is th eat in a french restaurant
where everything is presented well?
This is your chance! Remember, the
better it looks, the better it will
taste.

CLEAR SOUPS

Thin slices os lemons or oranges
chives
watercress
chopped green onions
podded peas
croutons (page 4)
Dumplings (page 5)
grated cheese

CREAM SOUPS

Sour cream
chives
croutons (page 4)
julienne strips of ham
parsley
chopped green onions

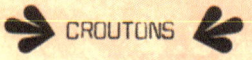 CROUTONS

I always use these two basic recipes.

1.  Saute bread cubes in butter and then season and let dry out a little.

2.  Butter pieces of bread and cut into cubes.  Put into oven, season, and leave in for about 1/2 hour on 200.

To season, shake on garlic salt, cheese salt, or onion salt.

## DUMPLINGS

Guess what?  I always use the old
standby, bisquick!  Actually, my
home made dumplings never turned out
well.  Make the dumplings and put in
some chives, chopped cooked onions,
or my favorite, cooked pieces of bacon.
HINT:
The secret to good dumplings is to
always keep them simmering on top.

## GREEN OR WHITE NOODLE DOUGH
### (OR FETTUCINI)

Roll out on pastry board or marble
table:

2/3 c. flour
1 egg
1 T. water
1/2 t. salt
1 t. oil

If you want green noodles add 2 to 4
T. very well pressed and dried finely
chopped cooked spinach at this time.
Roll dough for 10 minutes. Let stand
covered for 1 hour.  Now roll out with
lots of flour till very thin.  Let
dry another 30 minutes. At this point
you can hang the noodles over a piece
of foil or plastic. Then cut into strips.
1/8" for soups and 1" for lasagna.
Cooking time is 10 minutes. ( Green noodles
are very good served by themselves with
butter and grated cheese on top.

HINT:  Best not to make noodles in
         wet weather.

-6-

## BROWN STOCK

Take 2 lbs. lean beef, cut into cubes.
Brown slowly in 2T. melted fat and
drain and add:

2 qts. water

1 sliced onion

2 diced carrots

4 diced celery stalks with leaves

1 bay leaf

2 peppercorns

1 T. salt

1 mashed clove garlic

Cover and cook for about 1 1/2 hours. Now
strain very well.  Keep in frig so
you'll be ready for your next great soup!

SUPER
SUMMER
SOUPS

CHRISTINA ANN WILBUR

## CREAM OF CUCUMBER

Pare slice and peel:

2 cucumbers

Add to them:

1 cup water

3 slices onions

1/4 t. salt

1/8 t. pepper

Cover and cook this mixture till soft. Put in blender. Mix 1/4 cup flour with 2 cups chicken stock. Stir till smooth, add the cuke puree and 1/4 bay leaf and simmer for 2 to 3 minutes Strain and chill in a covered jar. Now just before serving, add 3/4 cup sour cream, 1 T. chives. Correct the seasoning and serve.

-8-

## QUICK BLENDER TOMATO

2-10 1/2 oz. cans condensed tomato soup
1 cup sour cream
snipped parsley
1/2 cup cooked chopped onions
seasonings
1 1/2 cup water

Put soup, sour cream and water in blender.
Puree till smooth, add onions.   Season
to taste.  Chill for about 2 hours or
more and garnish with parsley.  Not too
hard huh?

## GAZPACHO

Peel, seed and chop:

2 Large tomatoes

1 sweet pepper

Peèl:

1 clove garlic

Wash: (Have 1/2 cup or more of)

parsley

tarragon

chives

Put together and add:

1/2 cup olive oil

3 T. lemon juice

3 cups chilled water

1 sliced white onion

1 c. peeled seaded diced cuke.

1 1/2 t. salt

1/2 t. paprika


Some people prefer to use their blender
at this point.  I do not.


Chill and serve

-10-

## VICHYSSOISE

This soup can be served hot, or cold.
I, quite frankly like it both ways.

Chop and saute in 3 T. butter:

3 medium leeks

1 medium white onions

2 stalks celery

Add 2 cups water.

Add:

4 medium  diced potatoes

1 bay leaf

1 T. garlic salt

1/4 t. thyme

1/8 t. rosemary

salt and pepper

When poatoes are tender, thicken with flour.
Make pretty thick.  Now add 2 cups milk,
1/2 cup sour cream, 1/4 cups butter, and
at this point some wine if you like.
You can serve it with parsley now, or
put in a covered container and chill.
Always serve this soup with parsely.

HOT
HEALTHY
DEADWOOD
SOUPS

CHRISTINA ANN WILBUR

### CREAM OF ASPARAGUS

Take 1 lb. of asparagus and cut off
the tips.  Boil in small amount of
water till tender. Now cut stalks in
1/2" pieces and put in 12 inch pot
and simmer.

Add:

1 large white onion chopped

4 stalks celery chopped

1/2 t. rosemary

  "  "   thyme

  "  "   sage

1 T. garlic salt

add enough water to cover and simmer.
After tender, thicken with flour.
Next:  Take 1/2 mixture and put in
blender.  Mix both mixtures together
and add enough milk to thin. Add this
point add butter, maybe a little sour
cream.  Top with chives and serve.

## BEET BORSCH

Peel and chop:

1/2 cups carrots

1 1/2 cups onions

2 cups beets (diced)

Cover with water, simmer for 20 minutes

Add:

2 T butter

2 cups brown stock (page 7)

1 cup finely shredded cabbage

1 T. vinager

1 t. garlic salt

1/2 bay leaf

salt and pepper

Simmer for 15 minutes more and correct
the seasoning.

Place soup in bowls and add 1 T.
sour cream. Serve with pumpernickle
bread and drink beer instead of wine.

-14-

## NAVY BEAN SOUP

First decide how much soup you want.
Remember that navy beans swell to at
least three times their size when cooked.
Wash beans and cover with water. Simmer
making sure always to have the beans
covered with water. After about 1 1/2
hours, take 2 ham hocks, slice off
about 1/2 of the meat. Put the bones
in the soup. Chop up the other ham
and put that in the soup also.

Add a pinch of:

rosemary

thyme

powdered mushrooms (opt.)

garlic salt

salt and pepper

Now all you have to do is to simmer
till tender. This soup can also be
made in the crock pot. Slow and Easy.
Add butter before serving. This soup
is nice with sour dough bread, radishes,
celery sticks, carrot sticks and
cucumber slices. Oh, how about a bottle
of white wine also?

-15-

## CREAM OF CAULIFLOWER

Prepare 1 large cauliflower.
Cook and reserve water.
Saute in butter:

3 T. chopped onion

4 stalks celery, chopped

1/2 bay leaf

1/2 cup of reserved water

1/4 cup flour

Next:

take 1/2 of cauliflower and put into blender. Then add all engredients. Just before serving add about 2 cups milk, lots of butter, correct the seasoning. Serve topped with grated butter.

## CABBAGE

Very easy and you don't have to have
many engredients in your kitchen
to make it.
Saute till tender:
1 large white onion
2 T. butter
Grate and add:
1 small head cabbage.
bring to boil and add:
4 cups brown stock (page 7)
Add both together.
Season with:
Rosemary
Garlic salt
salt and pepper
Simmer for 15 minutes
Serve topped with sour cream and
bacon bits.

## CREAM OF CARROT

Saute till tender:
4 T. butter
1 large diced white onion
1/4 cup bacon pieces
2 cups diced carrots
Thicken quite thick with cornstarch
and then add:
2 cups milk
Take 1/2 of this mixture and put in
blender.  Add both together again.
Correct the sesoning, and turn on
low for about 20 minutes. Serve
topped with butter and chopped fresh
parsley.

-18-

## CHILE

I must admit, that this is one of the soups that my mother Dorothy made that really turned out quite well. I'm not saying that she couldn't cook, she could but this just happens to be one of her better dishes.

Saute in bacon drippings:

1 lb. ground beef

1 large sliced white onion

Pour into crock pot and add:

2 cups canned tomatoes (with juice)

2 cups canned kidney beans

3/4 t. salt

1 pinch thyme

2 to 3 T. chile powder (depending on taste)

1 mashed garlic clove

maybe some water to thin if you like

Cook in crock pot for about 1 1/2 to 2 hours. You will LOVE it!

 CORN CHOWDER

Saute till brown:

1/2 cup chopped salt pork or bacon

Addand saute till tender:

3 stalks celery

2 cups diced potatoes

2 cups water

1 large white onion chopped

1/2 bay leaf

1 mashed clove garlic

1/4 t. paprika

1 t. salt

Then add:

1/3 cup flour mixed witj 1/2 c. milk

2 to 3 cups whole kernel corn

1 1/2 cups milk

Be sure and not to boil after you've added the milk.  You also might want to add some sour cream.  I like to have oyster crackers with the soup.

## CLAM CHOWDER

In a very large pan put:
2 lg white onions, sliced
5 celery stalks with leaves
5 potatoes, diced
1 1/2 t. garlic salt
parsley flakes
salt and pepper
Cover all of these with water and
boil till tender
Add:
approx. 1/2 lb. cut up bacon pieces.
Thicken quite tick with flour.
Add:
cooked clams (as many as you like)
Add enough milk to thin
about 1/4 cup butter
a little white wine of course
Garnish with butter and parsley
and serve

CHICKEN AND DUMPLINGS

Go to the store and buy the can of
the 1 whole chicken, with broth.
Bone in a strainer so that you can
reserve all juice. Cut up the larger
pieces.  Put stock in a pan to
simmer  Throw in the chicken (no
skin)

Now season with:

1/2 bay leaf

1/4 t. thyme

 "  "   rosemary

 "  "   garlic salt

1/2 t. celery salt

salt and pepper

Add.

4 c water

Start to boil and throw in a few noodles.
Cook till tender then put in spoon-
fulls, the dumplings. (page 5)
Serve with hot rolls and butter.

## FISH SOUP

This soup I made in Mexico the day
after we had baked dorado. you can
also use this for shrimp. (very good)
It was baked (Chunked up) in cream of
mushroom soup and sliced onions. What
I did was, I took the bottom soup from
the pan, about 3 cups and heated it
in a pan very slowly.
In another pan, with enough water to
cover I boiled:
2 stalks celery, sliced
1 large white onion, sliced
2 large potatoes, diced
1 clove mashed garlic
1/2 bay leaf
Thicken with flour
Now add the 2 mixtures together.
Add enough milk to thin. Add butter to
taste, a little white wine and salt
and pepper. Super Soup!

-23-

## CREAM OF MUSHROOM

Saute in enough water to cover:

1 lb. sliced fresh mushrooms
1 large white onion, sliced
3 stalks celery, sliced
After tender add:

1 1/4 t. salt
1/8 t. paprika
3/4 t. garlic salt
1 1/2 cup water
about 1/4 cup bacon pieces

Thicken the mixture. Now, thin it with
milk.Do not boil after this point
Add about 1/3 cup butter, some sour
cream if you like,or maybe a touch
of wine also.
Serve with chopped parsley and croutons.

-24-

## FRENCH ONION

Saute in enough water to cover:
4 large white onions sliced
2 cloves mashed garlic
1/2 t. celery salt
1/2 bay leaf

After onions are tender add:
3 to 4 cups brown stock (Page 7)
salt and pepper
1/2 cup wine

When you serve this soup,be sure to add
mozarella or parmesan cheese to it.
Also put croutons (page 4) on top .
Hopefully you'll have more wine left.

## CREAM OF POTATO

Cover with water and boil:

4 to 5 cups diced potatoes

2 large wite onions, sliced

3 stalks celery, sliced

When these are tender, add:

1 1/2 cloves mashed garlic

1 bay leaf

1 pinch thyme

1 pinch celery salt

1 pinch powdered mushrooms

Simmer for 15 more minutes and then thicken
with a little flour. Simmer some more
and add milk, and bacon pieces if you
like.  Just before serving add a little
sour cream and top with parsley. When
choosing your bread for this soup,
why not try potato bread? Also in
each bowl, put about 1 T butter. It
makes the soup taste soooo gooood!

PUMPKIN

What a great fall soup. It's so
easy that you can whip it up in about
20 minutes. Very easy and very good.

Mix all of these ingredients together,
heat, but do not boil:

3 cups scalded milk
3 cups canned or 2 lbs. cooked fresh
pumpkin
1 T. butter
1 T. sugar or 2 T. brown sugar
Salt and pepper
pinch of saffron
1/2 cup julienned ham

Serve immediatly

-27-

## CREAM OF SPINACH (OR LETTUCE)

Wash 1 lb. spinach or lettuce.  Cook
for about 8 minutes and drain.  Put
1/2 of the spinach in blender and puree.

In saucepan melt.
2 T. butter
Saute till tender:
3 T. grated onion
Stir in 3 T. flour to thicken.
Stir In:
1/4 t. paprika
1/4 garlic salt
1/4 t. celery salt
salt and pepper
Slowly add 4 cups milk. Now add the
spinach puree and other spinach. Now add
lots of butter. I also found that putting
parmesan cheese on top is nice. A good
soup to have before the main course
because it's so easy.

-28-

## GRANDMA WILBURS STEW

My recipe may leave a little bit to
be desired. Don't get me wrong, it's
really good. I just mean that it's
hard to put it into cups, teaspoons,
and so on. You get the drift? O.K.,
here it is.

Get your meat together, I like to use
cubed round steak. Roll in flour and
brown in pan. Meanwhile,in another pan,
cover with enought water to boil:
diced potaoes, carrots, onions,and
chopped celery with leaves. Put this
mixture in a lage pot and to it add the
meat. Now add: 1 clove mashed garlic,
1 qt. canned tomatoes, 1 bay leaf,
small amount of tabasco,pinch chile powder
salt and pepper, and paprika. Simmer for
about 1 1/2 or 2 hours. You might want
to thin with water. If you want it
thicker, I add tomato sauce, or paste.
Serve with home made bread. It deserves
it.

## SPLIT PEA

In a lage pan, cover with water and boil:

1 16 oz. bag washed green peas

Always keep peas covered with water.

After peas start to swell, add:

2 white onions, sliced

1 pinch thyme

1 pinch rosemary

1 clove mashed garlic

1/2 bay leaf

1/4 t. celery salt

salt and pepper

After about 1 hour, take 1/4 to 1/2
of this mixture and put into the blender.
Put together again and simmer for about
30 more minutes.  Just before serving,
add your milk, some bacon pieces if
you like, or maybe ham. Correct the
seasoning, Put croutons on top(page 4)
and serve with sour dough bread.

## VICHYSSOISE

Surprise!  Just refer to page 11
and make it hot!  Serve with croutons
and sour dough bread.Oh, don't forget
the white wine. Heavy on the wine.

CHRISTINA ANN WILBUR

## VEGETABLE

Saute briefly in 3 T. bacon drippings
or fat:

1/2 cup diced carrots

3/4 cup diced onions

1/2 cup diced celery

Now add:

1 qt. canned tomatoes (with juice)

1/2 cup diced potatoes

chopped parsley

salt and pepper

pinch garlic salt

dash tobasco sauce

Cook for 45 minutes

add about 2 cups brown stock(page7)

Thicken if you like, and that's it!

## WON TON

I always buy the won ton wrappings, but you can make your own, (page 6) and cut in 4 " squares. Now, fix your filling (pork, chicken, veal, shrimp, or crab meat) Take about 1/2 lb. of one of these (cooked) and add to it:

2 finely chopped green onions
1 cup chopped spinach
1 egg, beated

Now, wrap in casings. Drop them in 1 gallon boiling water, add all at once.  Now, heat and when it starts boiling again, add 2 cups cold water to temper the dough.  All this should take about 10 minutes cooking time. Take 5 or 6 won tons and put them into a bowl.  Sprinkle on a little soy sauce, and pour over it,  chicken stock. To garnish, add a few cut chinese vegetables, or chives.

CPSIA information can be obtained
at www.ICGtesting.com
Printed in the USA
LVIW02n1907261113
362915LV00001B/15

* 9 7 8 0 9 6 7 3 0 2 5 4 6 *